Walt Disney, in a film made in the fall of 1966, describes for the first time his revolutionary vision of an Experimental Prototype Community of Tomorrow. Behind him is an early layout of Epcot.

I don't believe there's a challenge anywhere in the world that's more important to people everywhere than finding solutions to the problems of our cities. But where do we begin; how do we start answering this great challenge?

Well, we're convinced we must start with the *public need.* And the need is not just for curing the old ills of old cities. We think the need is for starting from scratch on virgin land and building a *special kind* of new community.

We don't presume to know all the answers. In fact, we're counting on the cooperation of American industry to provide their best thinking during the planning and creation of our Experimental Prototype Community of Tomorrow.

So that's what Epcot is: an experimental prototype community that will always be in a state of becoming. It will never cease to be a living blueprint of the future. . . .

Walt Disney
1966

Walt Disney's EPCOT Center

WALT DISNEY'S
EPCOT
CENTER

Creating
the New World
of Tomorrow

Text by Richard R. Beard

Harry N. Abrams, Inc.
Publishers, New York

Project Director: Darlene Geis

Editor: Lory Frankel

Designer: Dirk Luykx

Library of Congress Cataloging in Publication Data
Beard, Richard R.
Walt Disney's EPCOT.
1. EPCOT (Fla.)   I. Disney, Walt, 1901–1966.
II. Title.
GV1853.3.F6207432   1982   790'.06'80975924   82-3876
ISBN 0-8109-0821-2   AACR2
Special Edition

Published in 1982 by Harry N. Abrams, Incorporated, New York

Printed and bound in Japan

Contents

In the beginning was the plan: in 1966, Walt Disney and Card Walker (now chairman of Walt Disney Productions), surrounded by the 27,000 empty acres that will become Walt Disney World, including Epcot Center, study their blueprint for the future.

Introduction

Early in 1964, Walt Disney gathered a small group at WED (an acronym of Walter Elias Disney) Enterprises and began to visualize early concepts for Walt Disney World, including Epcot: Experimental Prototype Community of Tomorrow. The words were carefully chosen:

Epcot will be an *experimental prototype community of tomorrow* that will take its cue from the new ideas and new technologies that are now emerging from the creative centers of American industry. It will be a community of tomorrow that will never be completed, but will always be introducing and testing and demonstrating new materials and systems. And Epcot will be a *showcase to the world* for the ingenuity and imagination of American free enterprise.

Walt Disney's death on December 15, 1966, was a critical event for the company he had founded in 1923 with his older brother, Roy. His vision of "a new Disney world" outside Orlando, Florida, especially his concept of Epcot, was so strongly a personal, life-summing statement that many believed the dream might die with Walt. Not so. For in addition to the fantasy empire Walt had created, he had also built a unique organization.

Thus, when Walt died, the company went ahead with plans for the Florida project. Walt had said, "There's enough land here to hold all the ideas and plans we can possibly imagine." The first step was to establish a public focus . . . a place where people wanted to go to spend their vacations. To create these concepts was the responsibility of WED Enterprises.

Creative resources unique in corporate America to the Disney organization, WED and its sister manufacturing and production organization, MAPO (whose name comes from *Mary Poppins*, the profitable Disney film in release at the time MAPO was formed), are composed of a permanent staff of designers, engineers, artists, writers, architects, electronics and computer specialists, and many other talented people with dozens of craft and professional skills. Individually and collectively, they practice what we call "imagineering": the blending of creative imagination with technical know-how. Out of our rather free-wheeling, informally structured environment have come such widely diverse innovations as:

- "Audio-Animatronics,"® the system blending sound with animation and electronics to create lifelike three-dimensional performing human and animal figures.

- The Walt Disney World monorail system, which has carried more than 300 million passengers 5 million passenger miles in near-perfect safety

The artist's rendering of Epcot Center, following pages, shows the site when the stupendous dream is realized. In the foreground are the innovative buildings of Future World; across the lagoon, the national pavilions of World Showcase offer a convenient global tour.

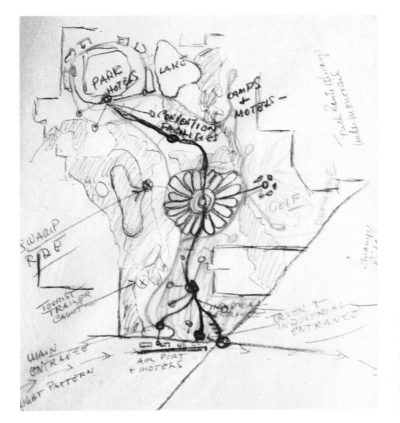

Disney's own early sketch at the left embodied many of the ideas that were adopted later in modified form as Walt Disney World became a reality. The rendering of Epcot Center, below, shows where each pavilion is located.

Africa
China
Germany
Italy
The American Adventure
Japan
France
Mexico
United Kingdom
World of Motion
Canada
Horizons
CommuniCore
Journey into Imagination
Earth Station
The Land
Spaceship Earth
Universe of Energy
The Living Seas
Monorail Station

- The WEDWAY PeopleMover, a linear induction-powered transport system introduced at Walt Disney World, certified by the federal government for city use, and now in its first public transit use at the Houston Intercontinental Airport.

- The DACS Computer Central, which controls and monitors (from a central source) all aspects of show performances "onstage" throughout Walt Disney World, from the opening and closing of theater doors to the singing of bears and birds and the speeches of pirates and presidents.

During the development of these new systems and concepts for Epcot Center, many media people, including Walter Cronkite and representatives of all three major television networks, visited WED.

When, in July 1975, Walt Disney Productions announced it was moving forward with plans for Epcot, to some it was a bolt of lightning to match the darting streaks that dance across the midsummer Florida landscape. The area had changed dramatically since 1967, when Walt Disney's film about Epcot was first shown to the State of Florida. No longer was the 27,400-acre Walt Disney World site—twice the size of Manhattan Island—virgin land with literally no amenities on its forty-three square miles.

There was now the whole Walt Disney World infrastructure that had been built in the intervening years: forty-three miles of winding drainage canals equipped with innovative flood control gates to maintain the flow and level of water; nine acres of underground corridors called "utilidors," a "city beneath a kingdom" that serves as an urban basement, providing vital operations and services—sewers, pipes, cables, workshops, garbage disposal—that keep the community aboveground running smoothly; revolutionary technical innovations such as the modular construction of hotel rooms, which are built on the ground and hoisted into place by crane; America's first all-electronic telephone system; the introduction in the United States of the Swedish AVAC trash disposal system, in which trash is funneled underground in pneumatic tubes to a central collection point; and many more forward-looking systems that will move urban technology into the twenty-first century.

What was lacking was a *public focus* for new ideas and concepts, a "center" for the communication of new possibilities for the future—directly to the public. To answer this need, we are developing Epcot Center: a permanent world's fair of imagination, discovery, education, and exploration that combines the Disney entertainment and communications skills with the knowledge and predictions for the future of authorities from industry, the academic world, and the professions. Our goal is to inspire the visitors who come here, so that they will be turned on to the positive potential of the future and will want to participate in making the choices that will shape it.

The pages that follow will describe in detail how each of the pavilions in Future World and in World Showcase evolved. As you read, and as you visit Epcot Center, remember that at our opening in October 1982 we are just getting started—there's much more to come!

Martin A. Sklar
Vice President
Creative Development
WED Enterprises

November 20, 1981

15

FUTURE

WORLD

After Walt Disney World opened in 1971, David Brinkley called it "the most imaginative and constructive piece of urban planning in America. . . . This is the future and . . . nobody has done it but Disney." One of the stops along the monorail that links Walt Disney World to Epcot Center is the Contemporary Resort Hotel. The entire Walt Disney World monorail system will have 14 miles of track when Epcot Center opens.

Whether you arrive by monorail or automobile, the entrance to Epcot Center is through the future. It is Future World that welcomes the visitor first, with the million-pound, 180-foot-high sphere of Spaceship Earth glinting in the sunlight, the largest structure of its kind in the world. Half a dozen pavilions form a wide ring around it, each dealing with an area of vital concern to all of us in the years ahead: energy, transportation, agriculture, mariculture, communications, technology—and imagination, without which advances in the other areas could not be made.

Each pavilion approaches its theme by giving us a look at where we were, where we are now, and what the possibilities for the future are. While some pavilions leap forward fifty or one hundred years, others emphasize that the technology available to us today will create the world of tomorrow—indeed, that the world of tomorrow is already upon us.

Epcot Center itself provides a brilliant illustration of the use of forward-looking systems and planning. The monorail system could serve as a model of transportation for cities; waste material from the park, as well as from nearby cities and towns, will all be burned to provide energy at an innovative pyrolysis (incineration) plant that will operate twenty-four hours a day; and the vehicles used in the Universe of Energy pavilion, powered partly by solar receptors on the roof, will move about, negotiate curves, and reposition themselves all through sensors that respond to wires in the floors, charging their batteries by induction at specified points without any electrical connections.

Nor will Future World remain static. Several displays are designed to incorporate advances as they come of age, and additional pavilions are planned into Future World's future. Horizons, a look into the twenty-first century, is scheduled to open in 1983, and a year later The Living Seas will join the ring of pavilions. Not yet in the building stage are Life and Health, which will conduct visitors on a journey through the human body, and a space pavilion, to be realized with the cooperation of NASA, which will feature a simulated space station.

It is the wedding of history, technology, and entertainment, all displayed in a setting quite unlike any other, that makes Future World unique. Each building has been designed to represent its theme in a style that is stunningly original while remaining appropriate to its subject. Behind each of these striking facades, where sheer fun accompanies the realistic and imaginative use of the technology of tomorrow, a new experience awaits us.

Water hyacinths are grown in one-quarter-acre channels, in sewage water from the main wastewater treatment plant. The hyacinths not only thrive on this diet, they also purify the water. In the process, they extract most of the nutrient from the effluent. Twice a month, a certain number of hyacinths are removed and placed on a compost pad; eventually, this will be used as a soil supplement.

In the Universe of Energy pavilion, we "ride on sunshine" in a practical application of solar power. In the Land pavilion, a ride through a growing area permits us to witness firsthand the latest breakthroughs in agriculture. In Communi-Core, we are encouraged to press computer keys, push buttons, become personally involved in the latest available technology. Similar "hands-on" experiences are part of the fun in Journey into Imagination, where we can share in the creative process. In our course through Future World we will see many films, but they employ so many different techniques—including a dozen never

Disney's world of the future is realized at last under the Florida sun: Spaceship Earth and the monorail are key elements.

before attempted—that after each film we will eagerly look forward to the next.

Enhancing the shows and rides are the startlingly lifelike Audio-Animatronics figures introduced in Disneyland and Walt Disney World. The "A-A figures," as they are called by their creators, are constructed of plastics in a Disney workshop. Outfitted with mechanisms that enable them to move convincingly down to the merest wrinkling of a brow, their faces and hands covered with realistic "skin," and their bodies clothed by the incomparable costume department in Disneyland, they are sometimes mistaken for the human beings or animals they represent. Their participation as "actors" in the various Future World presentations adds a touch of wonder to

the audience's enjoyment and stamps the shows with the unmistakable Disney hallmark.

Parades and pageants, frequently keyed to special events and holidays, enliven the public areas and walkways. The world of tomorrow is presented in a gala atmosphere that transforms formidable technology into something we can understand and look forward to enjoying.

While entertainment will continue to be a highly visible attraction of Epcot Center, it is the underlying educational value of Future World that is its most important contribution. Exciting, amusing, and fascinating as each pavilion is in itself, it is but an element of a project that may well be viewed as a springboard to our discovery of new worlds.

Spaceship Earth

Presented by the Bell System

It is, among other things, the world's largest geodesic sphere—not dome, but sphere. It started out, less ambitiously, as a dome—the world's largest geodesic dome, at that—but, happily, the bolder vision prevailed.

Now the sphere, 180 feet in diameter, rises some eighteen stories high—a stunning silver ball dominating the landscape for miles around, with little to rival its rotund majesty. Although at first sight it looks like nothing so much as a gargantuan golf ball on the putting green of the gods, it

Engineering solutions were worked out at WED on a carefully constructed model of a geodesic sphere, left. The geodesic forms pioneered by Buckminster Fuller a number of years ago became the inspiration for this newest, and by far the largest, such structure— Spaceship Earth.

An artist at WED, below right, paints a model to approximate the shiny facets of aluminum "skin" that will encase Spaceship Earth.

The real Spaceship Earth, right, dominates Epcot Center, and at night, when its facets reflect multicolored lights, the structure becomes a work of art worthy of Victor Vasarely.

The spectacular ride on a "time machine" that winds around and upward in the interior of Spaceship Earth takes visitors from the first images painted on cave walls, through the development of language and writing in ancient times, to Gutenberg's first printing press, on to the present marvels of television and motion pictures, and beyond to the future forms of communication. Every detail has been worked out, first with sketches, then with detailed small models and sets for the walk-through approximation of the full-sized ride.

takes on another aspect as we begin to appreciate its purpose—to reproduce the form of our spaceship, the planet Earth.

With an outside "skin" of an aluminum that is smoother than glass, the globe's facets reflect diffuse images as varied as its surroundings: by day, Spaceship Earth mirrors the sky, the land, the patterns made by Epcot Center's structures, walkways, and visitors; by night, it glints with the sparkle and illumination not only of World Showcase across the lagoon but also of the galaxies, the stars, the planets it emulates.

Epcot Center's engineering problems and solutions are as fascinating as the shows themselves. But many of the problems in building Spaceship Earth arose from the choice of a sphere as opposed to a dome, something that had never been done before. The concept stemmed from a desire to make a particularly dramatic entranceway, to give the effect of actually going up into Spaceship Earth rather than walking through a door in its side.

Once inside, we enter the realm of another team of designers, whose responsibility it was to create a show equal to the spectacular surroundings.

And so they did.

The theme show of Spaceship Earth treats of communications, a motif particularly appropriate not only to the pavilion's sponsor, the Bell System, but also to the Disney people, who consider themselves communicators above all. Specifically, the show presents the evolution of man's ability to communicate. For earliest man, it was a distinct advantage in assuring his survival.

The story of communications transmits a message at once profound, provocative, and promising. In a "time station," before the show begins, a narration sets the stage: Who are we? Where did we come from? Left with the suggestion that the answers begin in our collective past, we board a "time machine"—an open train of two vehicles, four persons to a vehicle—to begin a trip spiral-

Johann Gutenberg, the miraculous Audio-Animatronics figure at the left, is programmed to operate the printing press he invented. Here he is being fine-tuned so that his movements will be absolutely lifelike.

ing upward through the great globe itself and sweeping through forty thousand years of recorded time.

Now the vehicles move through the first of the ride's splendid sets: a cave dwelling. Fifteen minutes and 40,000 years later we get a glimpse of a thoroughly up-to-date communications center. People are running systems checks, calling up on a large terminal first a global view, then an electronic picture of the United States, then focusing in on central Florida.

We have entered the era of computers, machines that sort, store, sift, count; machines, the narrator reminds us, "whose billions of electronic pathways stretch to the very edge of space." We depart our trail through history and join them there, cruising into the dome at the top of Spaceship Earth, a vast planetarium where the heavens

Michelangelo will be shown creating his powerful Adam on the ceiling of the Sistine Chapel—but first a Disney artist, above, has to paint the fresco. Meanwhile, an ancient Egyptian bas-relief is faithfully re-created by a twentieth-century artist at WED, below.

are reproduced and some four thousand star effects might be shown.

From the vantage point of space we look back on the world—tiny, fragile, but very much alive, our own Spaceship Earth.

Beginning our descent—and passing on the way a crew of astronauts making repairs on a shuttle vehicle in outer space—we come down to earth, in more ways than one. We are, after all, fellow passengers on our Spaceship, and we are reminded that not only were the components of our infinitely intricate modern communications network created *by* us, they were also created *for* us.

Brief videotapes from around the globe demonstrate the practical, the human application of our advanced technology. They give a fleeting but telling impression: from bustling cities to remote islands, people's lives have been made healthier,

happier, safer, more comfortable, and more productive through the harnessing and dissemination of our collective knowledge.

With a last and rather awesome look at the current state of the art of communication—Landsat (satellites that survey earth resources) views of the earth; thermography; computer graphics and animation; microcircuitry; computer-enhanced images of ourselves and our environment; a veritable deluge of information—we are eased gently back into our "time station."

Somewhat spent after the compression of forty thousand years into a fifteen-minute tour, we are nevertheless exhilarated by the prospect of another forty millennia, and rather inclined to agree with the narrator's conclusion:

"Ours is the age of knowledge, the age of choice and opportunity. Tomorrow's world approaches, so let us listen and learn, let us explore and question—and understand."

Inside the entrance to Spaceship Earth, visitors will be greeted by a towering mural of a communications satellite, left, depicting man's conquest of space in the service of transmitting information.

A sophisticated communications center is operated by lifelike Audio-Animatronics figures.

Earth Station

Presented by the Bell System

In a park of the magnitude of Epcot Center, it can happen to anybody:

You've just come out of Spaceship Earth, and where do you go from here? It's all so vast, even a little intimidating. For you, then, and for all of us who come unraveled from time to time, there is Earth Station, also known as Epcot Center Information, adjacent to Spaceship Earth. It functions in effect as Epcot's city hall, with a little Times Square razzmatazz thrown in just for fun.

It is the city hall in the sense that this is where you come to find out what you need to know about the community of Epcot. Beyond that, the facility replaces the "Tickets and Information" booths that are spaced so strategically throughout Disneyland and Walt Disney World

What to do and where to go in Epcot Center? WorldKey Information Service answers your questions on touch-sensitive TV screens.

Replacing old-fashioned information booths, large video screens such as this one at Earth Station will give visitors a visual idea of what is available at Epcot that day. Visitors can request more specific information and make restaurant reservations at several touch-sensitive video screens.

and which, incidentally, dispense far more information than tickets.

At Earth Station, however, a number of those friendly people in the booths have been superseded by touch-sensitive video screens. It sounds forbidding, but even if you don't understand the first thing about computers, through curiosity, fascination, or maybe even out of desperation, you are going to walk up to one of those infernal machines, you are going to touch it in the appropriate place, and you are going to find out much of what you wanted to know.

Welcome to the twenty-first century!

What Epcot Center has done, without much fanfare, is to introduce you, innocently, gently, and entertainingly, to the new world of information, while never for a minute neglecting the human factor.

There are moments in everyone's life when even the beautiful simplicity of the video screen seems beyond one's capabilities. At such times, a single touch brings immediate assistance, live and in color. The Help Button operates on the theory that in a time of emergency, great or small, there is no substitute for person-to-person contact. If

your problem is not too serious, try to remember to smile: you're on Epcot camera!

Visitors to Walt Disney World may be already familiar with the screens installed there as a prototype in 1981, while future visitors may also find them in hotel rooms and lobbies. At Epcot Center, it is no coincidence that most of the terminals are located where guests disembark from Spaceship Earth, a pavilion devoted to communications past, present, and future. The designers had suggested to the Bell System (sponsor of Spaceship Earth) a post-show exhibit that, in addition to showing what the company was doing, actually provided a service that people could use on the spot—something really vital to visitors here and now.

Your forefinger will turn on the touch-sensitive terminals whose screens operate by means of an invisible grid of photo diodes and photo detectors. This WorldKey Information Service, developed especially for Epcot Center by the Bell System, provides special two-way video guest-relations assistance and will smooth your path through the park—once you can tear yourself away from the remarkable new plaything.

Artists' renderings and models have been faithfully transformed into the dim and eerie world of prehistory. Theater cars glide past Audio-Animatronics dinosaurs, while passengers traverse 275 million years in five minutes.

Universe of Energy

Presented by Exxon

The building, shaped like an enormous triangle with the apex tipped toward the ground, seems to rise out of the earth in a great swoop of silver and gray. With its unique architectural shapes and clean lines, it makes a dynamic statement, as well it should: it houses the Universe of Energy.

Among its more unusual features is the roof, laden with row upon row of photovoltaic cells, sparkling in the sun. These cells, 80,000 three-inch, wafer-shaped solar collectors, are arranged on the diagonal in 2,200 panels. All together, the photovoltaic cells capture power from the sun to generate about 77 kilowatts of DC current at peak sunlight conditions. This is converted to AC current to help run the pavilion's ride-through vehicles.

After entering the pavilion, we assemble in a pre-show area. Here, a spectacular multi-image presentation—live action and animation on a "magical" screen, accompanied by music—introduces us to the topic of energy with a review of its general principles.

Outdoors, a tree that looks at home in California is being properly aged, below, for the primeval scene. On an immense sound stage obtained from MGM, Disney artists, above, painted nearly 500 running feet of prehistoric landscape for the world of the dinosaurs.

Leaving the pre-show area, we proceed to Theater I to see an animated film on the formation of the fossil fuels—coal and oil. Our theater seats are actually "traveling theater cars." These vehicles, each holding 97 passengers, for the most part "ride on sunshine" as they transport us through the Universe of Energy.

Even though the special effects are dazzling, we never lose sight of the story—how the oil, coal, and natural gas so important to our way of life came into being.

This story acts as a perfect prelude to the next adventure—a journey through a fantastic primeval world. The doors of Theater I slide down into the floor, and our theater cars, now a train of vehicles, glide into the dark, damp ambience of the Mesozoic era—a world complete with swamplike sights, smells, and sounds.

It's dark in there, but as the sun rises we are reassured by the sight of a family of peaceful brontosauruses gathered at a pond. The baby of the clan plays with its mother's tail, and even when the father stretches his neck over the vehicles and spreads his jaws, the family scene holds little terror; we know they're vegetarians, and he is only chomping at the treetops.

The smell of sulfur heralds the spectacular end of our voyage and signals the end of the dinosaurs' world. With a great rumble and heaving, a volcano erupts, pouring out a flood of molten lava that flows toward us in a bubbling, scarlet stream.

It's a finale in yet another sense—the end of a billion years of the formation of fossil fuels. So, armed with a concrete and vivid conception of

A terrifyingly accurate model of Pteranodon, above, one of the last of the giant flying prehistoric reptiles, will give the Universe of Energy ride some thrills and chills.

Appropriately, Future World's Universe of Energy gets some of its power from the sun. The pavilion's roof is banked with rows of photovoltaic cells that trap solar radiation and convert it to electricity.

just how long it took to create the fuel we have been consuming so prodigally, we travel into Theater II.

The twelve-minute-long film records the toil, sweat, and ingenuity required to obtain energy. But it is not without its breathtaking scenes of rare beauty—a broad stretch of the Alaskan frontier, the Middle Eastern desert, the treacherous sea. These images convey a sense of man's nobility as he struggles to maintain and improve his life with the help of energy.

The film then brings us home to point out the use of the solar panels on the roof of the very building we're in. It's a true and optimistic demonstration of how sun power can be tapped.

Our theater cars begin to move again and we glide back into Theater I. But now the room looks different. Curtains have been raised to expose fully mirrored walls on two sides of a triangular space.

The show, titled "The Universe of Energy," is a dynamic reprise of the concepts of energy we've just seen. This is, in fact, the largest computer-animated film ever to be projected. In a kinetic presentation, set to music, images—computer-animated line drawings, glowing in radiant, laser-like colors—melt into new images and engulf us.

And as we leave, although we know the challenges are great, our spirits are lifted at the potentials and options that have been set before us in the Universe of Energy.

Assembling Tyrannosaurus Rex, king of the dinosaurs, was no easy task for four strong men at WED, right. Machinery in his body will be programmed to make him thrash and roar.

A technician in Special Effects, below, tests "molten lava," a harmless gelatinous material used in food additives to which orange dye and black-light pigment have been added for a fiery glow. The volcano will also shoot out appropriate sulfurous odors, courtesy of the WED "smellitzer."

Horizons

Presented by General Electric

The building that houses Horizons, like the future, can be interpreted in many ways. This ambiguity was intentional on the part of the designers, who wanted a structure that would gear the viewer's mind toward visions of the future. For that is the subject of Horizons.

Actually, it is a pavilion of the future in more ways than one: it will not open until October 1983. Significantly, it focuses less on technology than on a historically enduring social unit: the family. Rather than emphasizing the inevitable development and perfection of incredibly sophisticated machines of the future, Horizons concentrates on the purpose of the machines. And the purpose is us: how can our lives be enhanced by the future technology?

The city of the future, below, provides a variety of ways to get around.

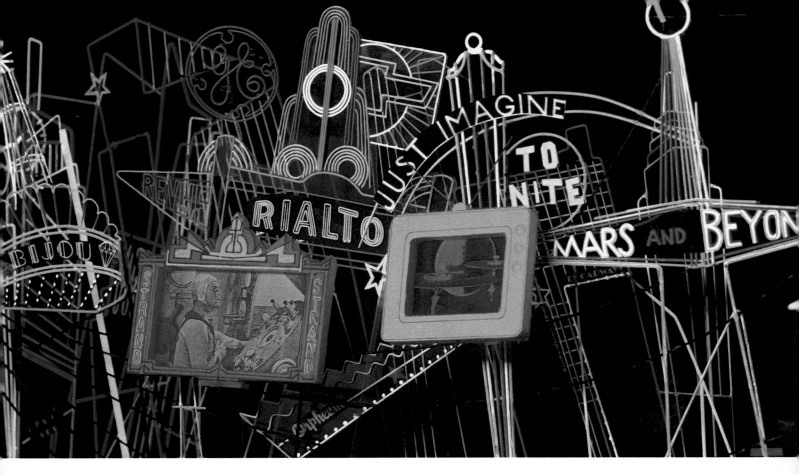

The Neon City will show clips from famous science-fiction films that deal with the future.

The Neon City sets a background for early movie and television dreams of the future; in one sequence, apartments on bridges above crowded neighborhoods foretell one solution to overpopulation.

In this first part of the ride, the point is made that people have always looked to the future. The difference today is that we're learning so much about our world through science and technology that we now have the skills to build our future in many ways. The future is here.

With that in mind, we move into the Omnisphere, the segment of the ride that deals with the present. Here we are confronted with two Omni-Max screens, each eight stories high and eight stories wide. It is the perfect medium to engulf us in the wonders of modern science and technology. Among the images planned for the Omnisphere are:

• astronauts practicing construction techniques

The model above shows the ''mechanical wonders'' envisioned fifty years ago: while a robot vacuums for him in the center of the room, the man at right reclines in a chair, having his hair cut and acquiring a remote-control suntan from the tropics.

In the underwater city of tomorrow, left, man, machine, and marine life coexist in peace. Above, a designer works on a model of the underwater observation tube for the floating-city sequence.

for outer space in the natural buoyancy of a NASA tank on earth;

- a computerized Landsat view of agricultural areas;
- a thermal cityscape changing shape and hue as infrared scans reveal invisible heat patterns;
- a thermal body scan, whose colored patterns reveal potential health problems;
- robots at work in manufacturing;
- a "flight" over a microscopic computer chip, highly magnified to reveal its intricate architecture;
- the Very Large Array (VLA) radio telescopes scanning our active universe;
- divers exploring our aquatic frontier in ultra-modern suits.

We visit a submarine city of the future and its environs. At surface level, there is kelp farming, which provides both food and fuel. On the bottom of the sea a robot harvester "vacuums" manganese-rich nodules from the sea floor.

In a dark tunnel, we make the transition to the

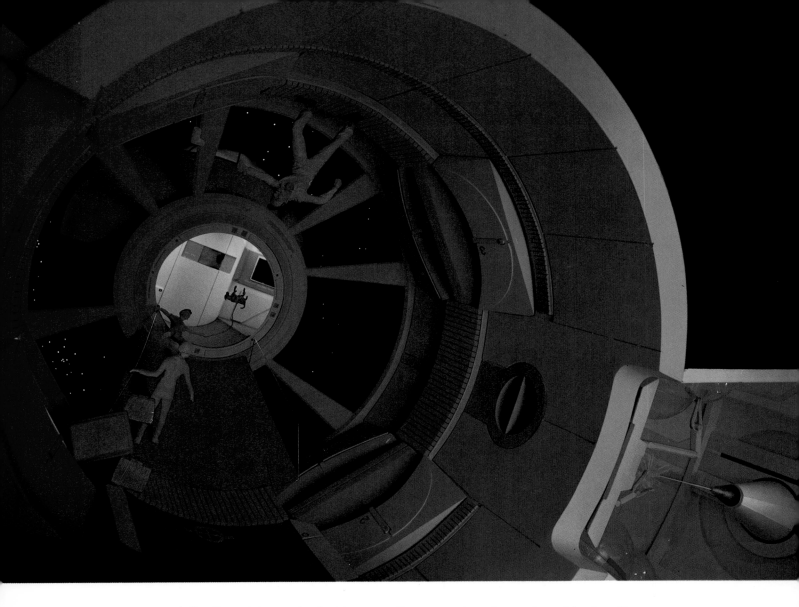

A family arriving at the docking port of a space colony is nonplussed by the effects of zero gravity.

next scene as the twinkling eyes of fish become stars in outer space. We find ourselves in the center of a spherical space colony, which revolves for gravitational reasons. To create it, the Epcot designers constructed a miniature spherical set, then photographed it from the center. It is complete with residences, roads, lakes, even an illuminated sports stadium, all visible in the distance.

One of the motives for colonizing space is to develop new industries that will produce materials superior to similar items manufactured on Earth. The manufacture of crystals, which can be grown larger and purer in space, is one of the most promising space industries. We are shown its possibilities in a scene of a zero-gravity "crystal farm."

We enter a "launch tube" and blast out into space, on our way back to Earth. Vehicle tilt, special sound effects, and high-speed simulations will combine to create an experience unlike anything visitors have had before.

As we leave the pavilion, we pass a colorful mural that encapsulates the whole show. It will certainly lead us to think back on all we have experienced in the pavilion, and to join our private visions of the future with those we have seen.

The newly arrived family will live in a space habitat like the one shown above.
Below is an appealing vision of a future city.

A busy space shuttle, pictured on the following pages, services the network of
communications in space.

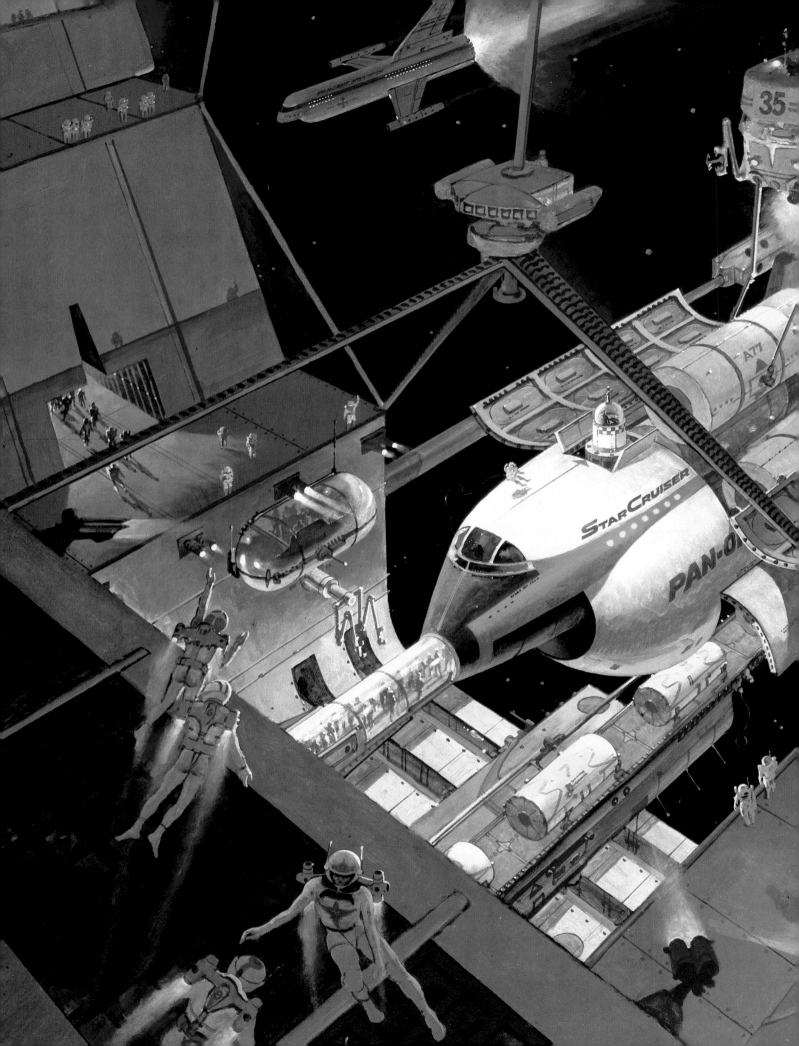

World of Motion

Presented by General Motors

Within the wheel-shaped World of Motion, above, the history of transportation is amusingly presented. TransCenter, on the ground floor, designed by General Motors, features exciting hands-on displays of automotive science, below.

With its perfectly circular form, this pavilion may remind us of a wheel, which is appropriate to a building that contains the World of Motion.

While the structure is firmly anchored to the ground, the show inside takes off in many directions. On the ground floor is the TransCenter, designed by General Motors, displaying examples of innovative and advanced concepts for present and future directions in transportation. Between the second and first floors, the CenterCore, a stunning evocation of a city of the future, uses the entire height of the building—sixty feet. Starting our tour on the second floor, we ride through a show that presents a refreshingly zany

The pig below is readied for its trip in a balloon, above, which heralds the "Age of Flight."

history of transportation—including its low as well as its high points.

In quick succession, we take a psychedelic trip in mixed media through the very first wheel factory and pass Egyptian, Chinese, and Greek temples to arrive at a used-chariot lot in ancient Rome.

The "Age of Flight" is heralded by an intrepid balloonist soaring over the rooftops of London, a cargo of pigs, goats, and chickens peering over the edge of the gondola.

"The world's first traffic jam" is a surpassingly glorious mess. In the main square of an American city of around 1910, a horse-drawn produce cart has tangled with a fruit peddler, with predictable

results. The street is strewn with vegetables and fruit, the round ones rolling crazily, the others crushed to a messy pulp. Backed up behind the wreckage are all manner of conveyances: a double-deck bus, an ice truck, a junk wagon, one of the new-fangled horseless carriages.

The grand finale is a "speed-tunnel" dash. Surrounded by filmed environments giving the illusion of pell-mell speed, we get to ride a snowmobile through a New England landscape, pilot a crop-dusting plane, hurtle down a steep-sloped bobsled run, and at last we slow down in time for an all-too-brief descent through the CenterCore.

When we "land," we're still in the future, and still moving, in a way. We are given the opportunity to "ride" in three bubble-type cars of the future, designed by General Motors and projected on a mirrored surface to give us the illusion that we are tooling along in our own twenty-first-century automobiles.

In Design 2000, we can marvel at this "future car." Moreover, all the steps that went into its construction are set out for us. Beginning with studies of the needs of the public and of safety and performance factors, the designers then made several sketches of the prototype car of tomorrow. The results of different tests influenced the models that were next built. In a full-sized "seating buck" displaying an advanced electronic dashboard, the driver sees all of the gauges as ghost images in the windshield, so he never has to take his eyes off the road.

Other displays include an amusing vaudeville turn performed by "The Bird and the Robot."

Guided by the small model in the foreground, designers, below, work on the full-scale set for a classic traffic jam in an early twentieth-century American city.

These Audio-Animatronics figures are being programmed from a computer to take part in a scene of a train hold-up from the history of transportation show.

The Robot, which represents the new robotic technology being used in car manufacturing today, is the brightest of the breed of animated performers—the first to pick up and set down props.

Changing exhibits that incorporate new ideas as they come in from all over the world will make the Dreamers Workshop a fascinating display well worth several visits.

In TransCenter's show "The Bird and the Robot," the robot (named Tiger) breaks into show business under the tutelage of the Bird. Tiger performs a variety of tricks for the audience, beginning with simple things such as rolling over and playing dead, and ending with a flourish as he conducts a symphony orchestra. In this storyboard drawing at right, the robot, who up to now has been quietly working wonders in automobile factories, has learned to demand his just rewards.

Journey into Imagination

Presented by Kodak

How do you house Imagination? Its architect conceived the main theme of its pavilion as two great crystals of truncated pyramidal shape, the pyramid being a form associated with the earth and its creation.

A more intimate and playful mood prevails in the Magic Garden that serves as a courtyard in front of the pavilion. Here, shrubs are pruned into whimsical shapes: animals and apparitions and other figments of the imagination. Fanciful fountains strike a pleasing note.

Inside the pavilion, we take a trip that mirrors the process of imagination. We get off to a flying start as we speed through the universe; at least, that is what we think is happening. In our seven-passenger vehicle, we are actually moving in a large circle, with our Audio-Animatronics host Dreamfinder flying along with us in his own dream-gathering vehicle.

Drifting past Dreamfinder's vehicle as it flies through the universe are animated "glows" representing ideas and inspirations. We are collecting these materials to take home where they will be recombined to make new things—inventions,

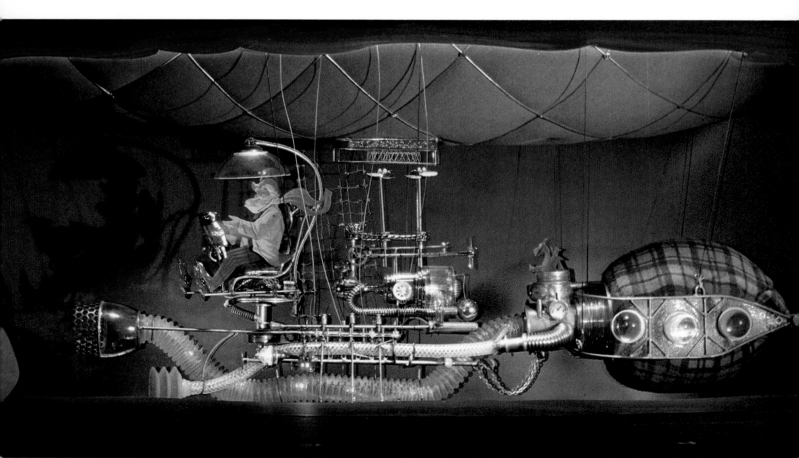

The pyramid shapes of Journey into Imagination glisten
in the sunlight in this artist's rendering.

Our hosts through the world of
imagination, Dreamfinder and
Figment, are portrayed as the
lovable characters they are in
this artist's rendering. Dreamfinder represents the spirit of
imagination, and Figment—who
is created before our eyes from
the materials of imagination—
embodies childlike spontaneity.

In a model scaled at 1″ to a foot, left,
Dreamfinder pilots the improbable-looking Dream
Vehicle, a contraption designed to gather ma-
terial for some later creative use.

Holding a pot of rainbow colors, Figment paints a fantasy landscape in the realm of "Art."

Ideas and images are sorted and stored in the Imaginometer, above right. The Dreamport storeroom, right, holds all of the elements of imagination, including a pigment-mixing machine, a diving bell for deep thoughts, and a box of "childish delight."

stories, songs, pictures, all the cunning contrivances of the imagination.

Notes are gathered from the air; sounds, shapes, and colors are sucked in. A combination of "horns of a steer, royal purple pigment, and a dash of childish delight" conjures up Figment, a little dragon. Figment is a spontaneous creature, full of energy and childlike wonderment.

"Can I imagine, too?" asks Figment. Can he! A passing rainbow is vacuumed up, and is transformed into a paint set for the dragon.

In a vast, busy storeroom—representing the brain—the booty of our expedition is being unloaded into appropriate containers: jars, drawers, cartons, a boiler-*cum*-washing machine called the Imaginometer.

From the Dreamport, our ride takes us into a series of spaces where the elements that were gathered and stored are recombined, each area featuring a new twist on a familiar theme—the very essence of imagination.

In a gentle reminder that with a little imagina-

tion we can all be what we want to be, Figment, poised in the center of a film reel, does his last little dance. Around him, filmed images of our indefatigable little guide, variously garbed as an astronaut, an athlete, an actor, a scientist, join him in synchronous song and dance.

The ride is so delightful and engaging that, when it ends, we are left with a compelling urge to create something. This reaction is spontaneous, but it is naturally provided for by the canny show planners. Immediately ahead is a magic hall called the Image Works, where we may try our hand at a wondrous array of the creative tools of the future, inspired by our Journey into Imagination.

One such marvel is Sensor Maze, subtitled "It Knows You're There," which provides an artistic fun-house experience. A tunnel of neon rings assigns you a personal color, which escorts you through the giant tube to the Vibrating Mirror. Among other oddities of the maze is the Lumia, a voice-activated light show in a giant sphere that responds to the pitch and modulation of your voice, and Stepping Tones, where your tread triggers not only color and light effects but weird and wonderful sound effects as well.

The Image Works is spectacularly successful in its goal—giving you a chance to express yourself in ways you'd never thought possible. You may become so absorbed in its myriad pleasures that, were it not for the promise of still another presentation around the corner, you would find it difficult to leave.

One of the experiences offered to the visitor by the Image Works is Sensor Maze, left, an artistic fun house whose attractions include Stepping Tones, where the pressure of feet sets off color, light, and sound effects.

In "Magic Journeys," we join one of the children as he romps through the magic landscape of his imagination. In one segment, the toys in his playroom grow and grow, larger than life, then take on a life of their own—and we find ourselves in a wonderful circus. A large measure of the film's magic is due to the use of three different 3-D systems. One of them, custom-made for Disney, is designed to give pictures of a clarity and wealth of detail rarely, if ever, seen before. The 3-D system simulates human vision by using two cameras, each recording the object from a different physical plane.

The final amazing sensation of Sensor Maze is the Digital Wall, on the following pages, which flashes colors at a touch.

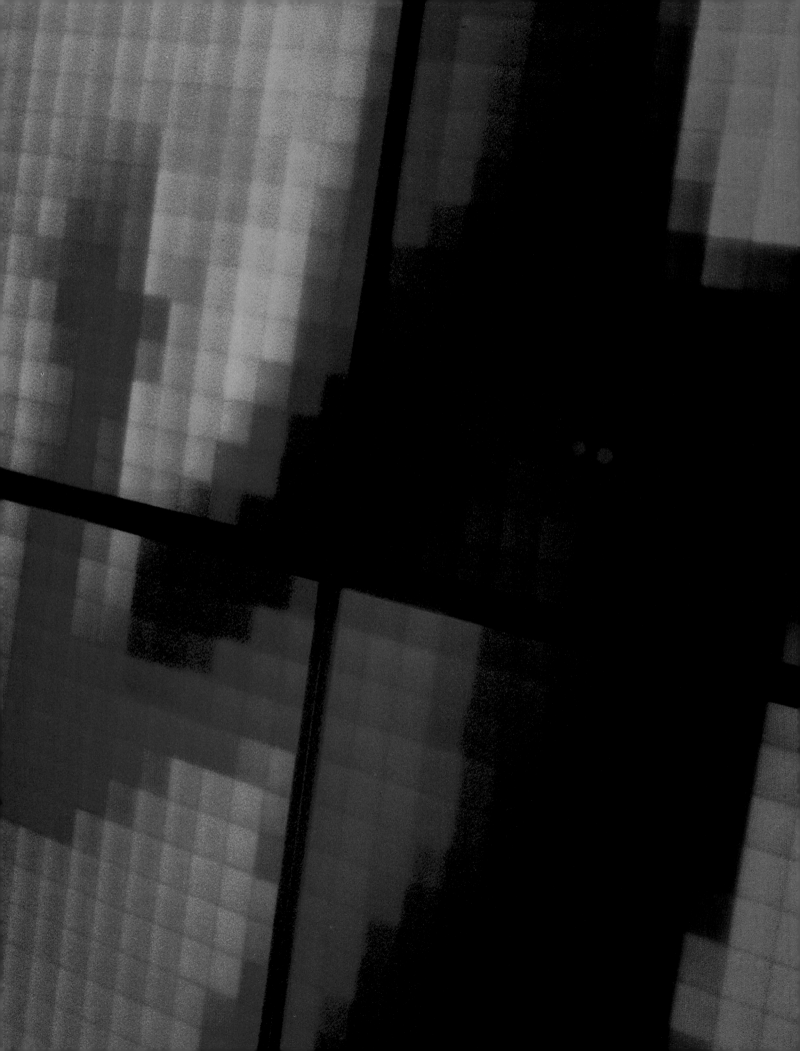

The Land

Presented by Kraft

It looks like the world's biggest greenhouse; now the largest of Epcot's pavilions, The Land covers six acres.

The members of the team that put together the pavilion get excited when they talk about it. The story of the land and its potential in partnership with man comes closest to the philosophy, purpose, and image of Epcot, according to the designers of the project. It's a story you can see, and touch, and feel, and even *eat!*

Allowing for their understandable bias, the elements of The Land still add up to a remarkable experience:

• A boat ride that begins with the exquisitely

A traditional American farm houses a theater where a film on modern American agriculture is presented. The boats are shown carrying visitors into the Barn Theater.

A cloud of balloons was released above The Land on its official opening; a gala crop scattered in the sky.

imaginative "Symphony of the Seed," then ventures into the various climates of the world before man, cruises through a turn-of-the-century American farm, and finally moves among actual growing areas for a mind-opening sample of agricultural techniques that are not only up-to-the-minute but that project into the future.

• A guided tour of the growing areas with detailed explanations of revolutionary methods of agriculture: hydroponics, intercropping, aquaculture.

• A surpassingly wacky, wonderful Audio-Animatronics revue called "Kitchen Kabaret."

• A moving and thought-provoking motion picture, filmed around the globe, on "Symbiosis."

On the boat ride winding through The Land, visitors explore nature—cultivated as well as wild—with a well-informed guide.

At the University of Arizona, whose Environmental Research Laboratory helped to conceive The Land's growing areas, a model of one such area is studied, below.

• Not one but two eating areas: a colorful Farmers Market for fast food, and a unique revolving restaurant where one can dine in style while surveying the ride area below.

Two boats at a time, each roofed-over boat accommodating twenty passengers, move through the "Symphony of the Seed." Conceived as a reminder that all life on Earth is based on the miracle of the green plant, it features projected illusions of seeds germinating, plants growing, fluids flowing, sun caressing, flowers opening, and fruits ripening.

The final segment of the ride is perhaps the most exciting: a live demonstration of modern agriculture. The Land has set aside three large buildings where actual growing takes place, but

The growing areas will employ advanced agricultural methods. Above is an example of intercropping. The luffa vines grow on bamboo A-frames, while soybeans and eggplants thrive below on the ground. Below, a worker lifts the polystyrene boards studded with lettuces to check the water medium—inhabited by aquatic animals—in which they are being grown, an innovative example of hydroponics.

New agricultural methods have enabled man to cultivate crops in hostile environments—even in outer space. This revolving drum reproduces the force of gravity, providing a down-home atmosphere for the plants growing inside.

no ordinary methods are used. The most innovative techniques are here put into practice, and, as soon as they become viable, new agricultural advances will be incorporated.

On display, for example, is a method of growing lettuce on polystyrene boards floating in a foot of water. Below swim fish who eat the lettuce roots yet do not stunt the vegetable's growth. Lettuce abhors direct sunlight, but there's a solution for that, too. Above the lettuce there are A-frames on which melons grow. The melons love sunlight, and provide shade for the lettuce.

Following the pattern of many of Epcot Cen-

ter's presentations, we've been guided from an uncertain past through an innovative present. Next we are given a glimpse of the promising future: a revolving drum that reproduces the force of gravity, thus creating an environment in which crops could be grown in outer space. A prototype constructed at the University of Arizona established the principle, but it took the engineers of Disney's own MAPO facility to perfect the model, a drum that will turn twenty-four hours a day, seven days a week.

"Kitchen Kabaret" is a rollicking show in the best Disney tradition; it has been compared to the

A model of the Boogie-Woogie Bakery Boy is being painted, above, as the Colander Combo looks on.

enormously popular Country Bear Jamboree at Walt Disney World. The show was developed because Kraft, a sponsor not without a social conscience, felt that somewhere in its vast and vital pavilion the story of nutrition should be told. So a trio of young and talented Imagineers was unleashed and encouraged to create a lively entertainment based on proper diet, of all things!

The mad and merry caper developed into a full-fledged cabaret turn with an introduction and finale sandwiching four acts, each focusing on one of the main food groups—dairy products, fruits and vegetables, meats and proteins, grains and cereals. Try to envision a mini-version of *That's Entertainment* as performed by a stalk of

An oversize stove for "Kitchen Kabaret" gets a paint job to match the small-scale model.

broccoli, a carton of milk, a loaf of whole wheat bread, and a can of grated Parmesan, and you begin to get the idea.

It's a giant shift in mood from "Kitchen Kabaret" to the Harvest Theater, but one worth making if we are to understand our relationship with the land—a partnership on which our very survival depends. The theater's magnificent film, "Symbiosis," deals with that mutually beneficial partnership. An altogether remarkable film, by turns harsh and sublime, it is, above all, provocative. Which way will we go? Will we conserve or waste, restore or ruin, use or abuse?

The choice is ours.

A designer adjusts the costume for Parmesan Cheese. He and Salsa are tasty members of the Kitchen Krockpots.

"Symbiosis," the film in The Land that shows how all things on Earth must coexist, records examples of human ingenuity improving on natural environments. In Holland the wind has been made to serve man.

The Living Seas

Presented by Walt Disney Productions

One of Epcot Center's most ambitious projects is The Living Seas, the pavilion dedicated to man's relationship with the sea. This involvement is most dramatically demonstrated in an enormous seawater tank that immerses us in the watery deep. The building itself, which conveys the organic feel of a huge shell, a monstrous wave, a palisade, sets the tone for the spectacle inside.

The show begins in a cavelike area where special effects eerily trigger man's atavistic awe of the unknown deep with the sensation of an approaching storm. The "wall" of the grotto gradually closes behind us as the storm reaches its full fury.

Inside the shell-like structure of The Living Seas, above, a surprise is hidden. The early cutaway view of the pavilion, below, reveals the "underwater" tank in the center.

In the research area of the pavilion, visitors watch divers preparing to enter the tank. Observation modules enable visitors to follow the divers' activities once they are inside the tank.

At length, out of a lightning bolt appears Poseidon, the Greek god of the sea, who will be the narrator for the rest of the journey to the Coral Reef.

The underwater setting is realistically furnished with the actual fish, rock forms, and plant life appropriate to a Caribbean locale—including live sharks! The environment, designed to look like a futuristic sea base, is an actual working environment in which man and machine coexist with the sea and its original inhabitants. All around us, we see divers carrying on their tasks, often accompanied by their coworkers, the dolphins, trained to work alongside man.

Once the ride is over, a television system enables us to continue to follow the divers' activities: one camera is set in place on the sea floor,

another is mounted on a robotic device following the diver, and a third, either hand-held or affixed to the diver's helmet, focuses in on the work at hand.

In four "undersea" modules, each concentrating on a particular aspect of the activity going on in the tank, we zero in on specific developments predicted for the world of the year 2030.

As in The Land, at the conclusion of our expedition through The Living Seas, we will be able to return to an "observation module" to pursue at our leisure any aspects of the show that have aroused particular interest. Among other exciting possibilities, we will be offered a guided tour of the life-support systems that maintain the base underwater—the vital underpinnings of this dramatic presentation.

The artist's rendering depicts Sea Base Alpha as visitors will see it, complete with divers, marine life, and observation platform.

CommuniCore

Technology, meet the people. People, meet technology.

Far from being forbidding, CommuniCore—short for Community Core—is an inviting group of interactive exhibits designed to take the mystery, but not the thrill, out of technology.

Like Earth Station, located nearby, CommuniCore not only welcomes guest participation, it solicits it. How can we resist the seduction of a pavilion where we may:

- Talk to a computer—and have it answer us.
- Contribute our own opinions on current issues to an ongoing poll—and actually have someone take notice.
- Check out our next travel destination as if we were scouting the place on the spot.
- Design our own concept of a Utopian community.
- Experience what it's like to pilot a space shuttle through reentry into the Earth's atmosphere.
- Control the pace and rhythm of our own downhill ski race.

Many of these adventures are ours for the choosing on opening day, and there is no telling what others will eventually be available, since CommuniCore is designed to be in constant flux. If there is one constant common to all technology, it is that technology is constantly changing. And with this expandable structure, built to accommodate ever changing exhibits, Epcot Center intends to keep up with the times.

Located at the hub of Epcot Center, in two structures that curve around Future World's main plaza, CommuniCore also serves a central function. Besides complementing the experiences offered by the other major pavilions, such as Uni-

verse of Energy, The Land, or World of Motion, it provides information pertinent to many aspects of our lives, helping us to make our own decisions. The aim of CommuniCore is to answer at least part of the question that troubles so many of us today: "How can I cope with this business of preparing for, participating in, and shaping the future?" To try to get the answers, we can spend as much or as little time in CommuniCore as we wish.

The focus of the presentations is the relevance of technological advances to our lives. The designers have taken the most prominent and convincing examples of where the future already is making itself felt. Seeing these examples in a concentrated space, we become aware of how much of what we take for granted is due, directly or indirectly, to advances in technology. We recognize that technology leads to more efficiency, even creativity, and gives us more choices, allowing us to exert better control over our lives.

The whole of Future World tells us, in effect, that the future is not something to fear, but rather is something to be desired. We can shape it the way we want it to be. Whereas some of the other pavilions try to speculate about the world fifty or a hundred years from today, CommuniCore shows us the here-and-now and the just-around-the-corner. It represents our first footsteps into the future.

Epcot Computer Central
Presented by Sperry Univac

It is the computer that makes this brave new technological world go round, and the computer is the star of Epcot Computer Central. From a glassed-in balcony, we see all the computers that run Epcot Center in action, as well as the crew of technicians who run the computers.

The functions of the computers are legion and astonishing to contemplate. Overhead screens help demonstrate the computers' long reach: they are instrumental in the precise running of shows, efficiently carrying out the orders of the computer programmers to record and play back elements of the shows, monitor the shows as they run, raise and lower curtains, operate the lights, control the sound effects—they even help in programming the Audio-Animatronics figures. In addition to their entertainment operations, they are integral-

Visitors find it pleasant to stroll in Showcase Plaza, below, where CommuniCore exhibits include Bell System's Fountain of Information in FutureCom, above.

ly involved in fire protection, security, energy management, reservations by the millions, and control of the attractions and ride systems.

Perhaps more than in any other exhibit, the sight of these machines at work brings home to us how vital and creative a tool the computer has become, and how many possibilities for the future it has opened up.

Energy Exchange
Presented by Exxon

Energy Exchange ties in directly with Universe of Energy. If you have been provoked or stimulated by the show in Universe of Energy and want to obtain more information on nuclear fusion, conservation, synthetic fuels, or any other energy-related topic, this is the place. It is organized in such a way that if you are interested in just one aspect of energy, you can immediately spot and head for the area of your interest.

Those not seeking in-depth information will be entertained by a number of devices whose performance depends on the viewer's input. In Video Bicycle, visitors pedal a stationary bike. The increasing brightness of the rider's image on a television screen shows just how much power a person can generate; soft-pedaling here won't get you across. Driving Machine, in which visitors take an automobile trip, graphically demonstrates how much the number of miles per gallon of gas varies according to speed, acceleration, use of air conditioner and/or power steering—optional factors that affect a car's fuel efficiency.

It's really an electronic library, offering something for everyone.

Electronic Forum

From the assembly of the ancient Greeks to the New England town meeting, every democratic community has had its forum, a place to meet with one's peers to discuss events of the day and to plan a course of action for tomorrow. In a very real sense, Electronic Forum is as lively and democratic as Athens's agora, and infinitely more efficient.

Once inside the theater, the audience of 170 is directed to the touch-button console in the arm-rest of each seat. Here we will register our opinions on a number of broad subjects—taxes, energy, care for the aged, education—as well as timely issues in the areas of defense, welfare, and whatever else is uppermost in people's minds at polling time.

FutureCom
Presented by the Bell System

The theme of another CommuniCore exhibit is the Information Society, a display mounted by the Bell System. Here, familiar as well as brand new communications techniques used in our everyday lives, at home, at work, and on the move, are treated humorously and informatively.

The giant Fountain of Information, the display's centerpiece, is almost a show in itself. Spilling out from the structure are elements of many different information media, keeping us busy identifying rolls of newsprint, traffic lights, computer printouts, sprays of tapes, cascades of magazines, film, and assorted information.

The Age of Information is a diverting attraction where large animated figures amusingly illustrate the benefits of an electronically equipped home, office, and transportation of the future.

TravelPort
Presented by American Express

In TravelPort, sponsored by American Express, we may journey, via videodisc, to the destination of our choice. Window-shopping on a grand scale, this method enables us literally to look into future vacation possibilities and scout the territory beforehand.

WORLD

SHOWCASE

World Showcase, curving along the shores of the lagoon that connects it to Future World, is a permanent community of nations whose pavilions stand side by side in exemplary amity. Mexico, China, Germany, Italy, Japan, France, the United Kingdom, and Canada are good neighbors to one another and to The American Adventure, the host pavilion located at the center of the group. Possibly one of the reasons there is no international disharmony is that all of the foreign countries have equal waterfront footage.

The visitor to Epcot, putting the hero of Jules Verne's *Around the World in Eighty Days* to shame, can take a miniaturized trip around the world in three hours, pausing to snap a picture of the Doge's Palace and campanile in Venice, Italy, the Eiffel Tower in Paris, France, a garden and Shogun's castle in Japan, and similar famous tourist sights at the other pavilions.

While The American Adventure is housed in a single structure, a magnificent Georgian mansion, the other pavilions have buildings, streets, gardens, and monuments that are designed to give the visitor an authentic visual experience of each land. In truth, after a tour of the World Showcase countries, you feel that you have really "been there."

A battalion of Epcot designers and architects has re-created entire mini-towns, complete to the last detail of the least roof, while commercial firms from the participating nations have stocked a broad variety of shops with enough merchandise to satisfy the most avid shopper or browser. Everything sold in the pavilions' shops has been made in the countries represented.

Restaurants, meanwhile, offer the cuisines of many lands, and a German beer garden and a British pub provide sustenance of another kind. Moreover, the pavilions have their own shows or rides, giving yet another dimension to the tour. Of particular note are the film presentations in China, Canada, and France, while a boat ride through the history of Mexico is one of the liveliest and most colorful presentations in Epcot Center.

Artisans, artists, and performers, dressed in traditional costumes of their country, add life and zest to the pavilions: a mariachi band strolls through Mexico; an Italian puppet show will enthrall visitors to Italy later in the season; lumbermen from Canada's great timber and logging areas demonstrate their skills in rip-roaring style; troubadours from Merrie England serenade visitors on ancient instruments, and Cockney buskers in pearl-buttoned costumes entertain passers-by with sidewalk comedy in the United Kingdom. In France, on the streets of Paris, crowds are amused by the antics of white-faced mimes in the tradition of Marcel Marceau; artists on the Left Bank paint and sell watercolor views of their romantic city; folk dancers from Brittany and Provence perform in their bright regional costumes.

The entertainment in Japan is entrancingly exotic. To music that falls strangely on Western ears, a troupe of Japanese folk dancers moves in serene and stately steps; a man selling rice toffee candy from his cart dances while he snips it into shapes resembling herons and dragons for the delighted crowd; a flower arranger creates works of art from a few blossoms; a parade featuring Japanese dolls and kites enlivens the streets and squares.

In China, a great dragon animated by dancers underneath its silken body snakes its way through

the pavilion, joined by the laughing crowds; a venerable Chinese calligrapher will inscribe a souvenir scroll with our names written in Chinese for a small fee while we watch. In Germany, a master woodcarver yodels while he works; alpenhorns, glockenspiels, cowbells, and the music of the Oktoberfest sound merrily throughout the pavilion.

The broadening effects of tourism work two ways. Not only are Epcot's guests introduced to the cultures, customs, crafts, and foods of other lands, but on the staff of each pavilion are about a dozen young men and women from that country, giving them a chance to meet Americans and other nationals. Through a program called World Showcase Fellowships, these youngsters from participating countries are brought to Epcot Center not only to work but to participate in an international community certain to enrich their outlook. They take part for a year in the community as employees, and also as favored guests.

During the entire year, the Disney entertainment division will focus on particular festivals of the various World Showcase countries, sometimes for a day or two, on other occasions for as long as a month. Countries not represented at World Showcase also have been invited to participate, in an effort to create a broad international ambience. In addition, once a day a Festival of Nations parade circles the perimeter of the lagoon.

But it is at night that World Showcase promises to be at its most seductive. With dramatic stage lighting illuminating the famous international landmarks, and with a concentration of fine dining facilities probably unequaled in such a small area anywhere in the world, a stroll through World Showcase will prove irresistible. A spectacular show mounted on a convoy of barges cruises the lagoon's waters, presenting filmed extravaganzas and firework displays for the people on the shores.

As the evening draws to a close, the crowds drift toward the American Adventure pavilion where dancers and musicians from all the other countries gather for a sensational international pageant in the America Gardens amphitheater. Against the backdrop of World Showcase Lagoon and the gleaming pavilions of Future World, the single large company unites in songs and dances that form a stirring finale to the day's adventures at Epcot.

In time, many more countries will choose to become a part of World Showcase—the possibilities are virtually limitless for the establishment of a true community of nations at Epcot Center.

The American Adventure

The centerpiece of World Showcase is The American Adventure, housed in this handsome Georgian building. From the model being painted in California, above, to the completed structure in Florida was a giant transcontinental step.

The American Adventure pavilion, at once stately and inviting, makes the visitor feel at home while conveying a sense of grandeur. The goal of the architect was to give the impression that this is America's mansion.

This, too, was the intent of the designers of the show that takes place in the mansion, and how well they succeeded! It was not an easy task, especially in view of the restrictions imposed by logistics, restrictions most notably including a running time of only twenty-nine minutes.

One could hit just the high spots, of course. But what about the low spots? There's no denying the practice of slavery and the ensuing carnage of the Civil War. There's no denying the Great Depression, the Vietnam conflict. Should one simply wave the flag, gild the lily, damn the torpedoes? Even given what must surely, and appropriately to The American Adventure, be an upbeat theme, can one ignore the tragedies of John F. Kennedy and Martin Luther King? Can pollution and crime be expunged from the collective American conscience, even for twenty-nine minutes?

And if you ask yourself why they didn't include this, how they possibly could have ignored that, you won't be alone. The Disney people themselves have been asking the same questions for years, since they first conceived the show, subsequently reworked a thousand times. But, chances are you won't be posing the questions at the end of the show. Chances are you'll be too stunned by what you see and hear. And, yes, inspired.

For The American Adventure, given the restriction of twenty-nine minutes, is quite simply the best story of America ever told.

The decisions that the Imagineers were faced with were staggering. Inclusion of certain scenes and historical figures was, of course, mandatory:

Our hosts in The American Adventure's dramatic trip through this country's history are Benjamin Franklin and Mark Twain, two remarkable Audio-Animatronics figures. The talking heads of our hosts, and of humorist Will Rogers, are being programmed for sound and action, left. Preliminary sketches and paintings, above, guided the sculptors.

The American frontier was pushed westward thanks to the pioneering spirit of men like this buckskin-clad explorer, who daringly opened up new territory.

the Boston Tea Party, the victorious world wars, the moon walk; George Washington, Susan B. Anthony, Neil Armstrong.

Who, finally, should narrate the show? Ben Franklin and Mark Twain were early favorites, and indeed lasted the course, Franklin for his cheery gifts of insight and invention, Twain for his more cautious approach couched in wry humor, the perfect foil for the irrepressibly optimistic Ben. Ben and Mark hold the show together, remarkable figures who talk and gesticulate, and in Ben's case, even walk.

As the lights fade and the show begins, Franklin speaks first, stating not only the theme of the show but the theme of America:

"America did not exist. Four centuries of work,

bloodshed, loneliness, and fear created this land. We built America and the process made us Americans. . . . A new breed, rooted in all races, stained and tinted with all colors, a seeming ethnic anarchy. Then, in a little time we became more alike than we were different, a new society, not great, but fitted by our very faults for greatness."

The Boston Tea Party leads inevitably to the Declaration of Independence. Ben Franklin climbs a flight of stairs for an eminently human chat with Thomas Jefferson, whom he finds laboring over a draft of the document in a Philadelphia attic. A musical bridge appropriate to the period sounds over Jefferson's reading from the Declaration, introducing the war it inspired.

The war won, America begins to flex its mus-

cles, commencing the push westward on the bent but proud backs of its doughty pioneers, men and women of every origin and hue. At the same time, a few courageous black slaves hazard a more desperate journey—a journey north to freedom.

Twain is with us again while Alexander Graham Bell and Andrew Carnegie introduce us to a Parade of Inventions marking yet another frontier: the frontier of ingenuity. Engravings of great inventions of the era (including the light bulb, the steam tractor, the vacuum cleaner, Edison's phonograph) are ingeniously animated in a se-

In an exciting film sequence, left, the World War I aerial dogfight between Eddie Rickenbacker in his Spad 13 and a German ace in a Fokker Triplane is reenacted.

The rural general store, below, appears in The American Adventure sequence that concerns the Depression of the 1930s. The Audio-Animatronics figures are being programmed for words, action, and banjo music.

Twain and Franklin, on the platform beneath the torch flame of the Statue of Liberty, wind up their tour through American history with Thomas Wolfe's hopeful words about the American promise.

quence concluding with the flickering image of an early Wright Brothers flying machine—the show's first motion picture—signaling the wings of change overtaking America.

But America's path to progress is erratic. Eleven years after its victory in World War I, the country is plunged into a severe economic depression. Several bowed but unbroken characters relax on the porch of a run-down gas station-*cum*-general store, keeping their spirits up with rueful jokes about hard times. A radio is turned on, and a strong voice offers hope: it becomes evident that no nation, however despairing, could possibly have hit the depths, with no hope of recovery, and still have spawned a president with the strength of Fránklin D. Roosevelt. The stage darkens, and Roosevelt appears. He appeals to the courage and determination that

run through America's history ("the only thing we have to fear is fear itself"). Rosie the Riveter, one of tens of thousands of women across the land to enter into the defense effort, takes a short break from patching up a war-pocked submarine to chat with a sailor on leave.

A collage of images brings us from World War II to the present. We see a vast sky, alive with vaporous colored clouds. As in a daydream, the clouds begin to assume shapes.

Predawn New York, its fabulous skyline in silhouette, fills the screen. Then the glowing torch of the Statue of Liberty takes the stage.

On a platform ringing the torch stand Ben Franklin and Mark Twain, pondering America's past and addressing themselves to America's future, with concern and with some criticism, but also with confidence and, above all, with hope.

Canada

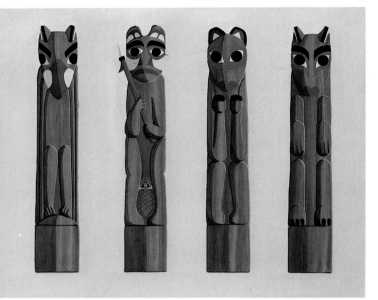

Canada's Northwest Coast is the home of a uniquely artistic Indian people, whose totem poles represent their family trees. The Indian Trading Post sells many Indian artifacts and exhibits others.

It is no coincidence that the first thing our eyes light upon if we travel up the right side of the lagoon is a superbly landscaped garden, the front yard, as it were, of the Canada pavilion. The pavilion designers consider nature to be the essence of this beautiful country.

The brilliant burst of flowers is fringed on the right by a stand of Canada's beloved maple trees. To the left, flanking the pavilion's entrance, is a stand of conifers—cedar, fir, and a sampling of some of the 650 species of tall trees found in northwest Canada. Beyond, in a marvel of forced perspective, rises a mountain symbolic of the country's rough-hewn grandeur.

It is a quintessentially pacific vista of the natural world, rendered no less natural by the

The Hôtel du Canada's French Gothic majesty rises behind the formal Victoria Gardens where visitors stroll and admire the brilliant flowers.

knowledge that the mountain actually houses a CircleVision theater.

We visit a street where French Canada is represented on one side and English Canada on the other. As we leave the urban area, the road narrows until we are heading down a little canyon, and then we cross a bridge to Salmon Island.

No, no salmon there; not even the Disney wizards could arrange that! Instead, a thirty-foot waterfall cascades into a lake from which a whitewater stream rushes through a gorge.

It's a bit of Paul Bunyan country, if indeed one can miniaturize a legend of such mammoth proportions, and here an appropriate show captures our fancy. Woodsmen smaller than Paul, but with no less determination, compete in the time-honored games of the great forest: log-rolling, tree-climbing, axe-throwing.

With some reluctance we move on, into a pre-show area cleverly designed as the Moosehead Mine, until it is time to enter the theater under the mountain to see "O Canada!" in CircleVision 360.

From the front screen, a troop of Mounties welcomes us to the show; as they ride around us, each screen comes to life in turn, the sounds of the band and the horses' hoofs following the images until each of us has the distinct and ego-gratifying impression that the entire ceremony is somehow centered on us.

Scene upon scene draws us closer into the country: now we are inside Montreal's magnifi-

A *CircleVision camera photographs band players for the changing of the guard in front of Parliament in Ottawa, above. When the movie is shown on a 360-degree screen, with digital sound, the audience feels surrounded by the band and its music. The film also offers the thrill of a white-water raft race from Montreal to Quebec, below.*

The Canada pavilion on a night of celebration, opposite.

cent Cathédral de Notre-Dame, moving up the aisle, surrounded by choirboys, as the sonorities of the great organ, captured in digital sound, delight the ear and stir the blood; now we are in the midst of thousands upon thousands of Canadian geese, taking off for parts known only to other Canadian geese; now we follow a speeding train along a river, leaving the train to soar over the snow-capped Canadian Rockies, which rival the Alps; now we are at the legendary Calgary Stampede—no, *in* it, actually in a bouncing buckboard competing in a mad race for glory, in the thick of the noise and whirl and fun that make the stampede the classic event of the North Country.

And if it's possible for mere film to capture the heart and soul of a country, this one does it.

France

As you enter the France pavilion, you have a last chance to walk over the Seine River in Paris on a footbridge. In fact, it's your only chance, even if you later go to Paris, because they've torn down the old footbridge that used to lead from the Louvre to the quais of the Left Bank.

Once in the pavilion, however, you may wonder for a moment just exactly where you are.

Are you in Paris? Yes.

Are you in the rest of France, known collectively as the provinces? Yes again.

Epcot Center has given you a little of both. Facing away from the lagoon (or from the Seine, if you prefer), you will find Paris on the right-hand side of the tree-lined boulevard, called La Promenade, that bisects the pavilion grounds. To the left, up a little street aptly named La Petite Rue, are the shops—not to mention the sounds and smells—of a provincial village.

Sidewalk cafés? Of course.

Don't linger, though. Paris is one of the great cities of the world for walking, and the World Showcase scaled-down version, while just as charming, is easier to cover on foot.

Chimney pots punctuate the rooftops in true Parisian style, and looming in the distance, high

All the charm and romance of Paris and the French provinces are conveyed in this rendering of the France pavilion. With the Eiffel Tower as its landmark and outdoor cafés to tempt the footsore tourist, this will surely be one of the favorite stopping places in World Showcase.

Step across the bridge, above, and miraculously you are in Paris! Au Petit Café, right, is the quintessential Parisian sidewalk café where you can linger over refreshments while watching the passing scene. But don't miss the serious dining indoors at Les Chefs de France. Paul Bocuse, Roger Vergé, and Gaston Lenôtre, three of France's most brilliant culinary stars, left, have created special dishes to be served there.

above them, is that symbol of "Gay Paree," the Eiffel Tower. At least the tower *appears* to be in the distance. It is a minor miracle of perspective. Constructed to scale from the actual blueprints of Gustave Eiffel himself, complete even to its little elevators, the tower rises a mere hundred feet.

Entering a building that recalls the classical facade of the Madeleine, you pass into an exquisite little theater similar to the one at Fontainebleau. It is actually a cinema of intimate proportions where a film on France will be shown to audiences of up to 350.

The miracle of broad-screen projection transports the audience through the chateaux of the Loire Valley; down the bustling street of a medieval town; high above the verdant countryside in the company of hot-air balloonists; into a vineyard at harvest time and among the field hands gathering the grapes; down a river by canoe; perilously close to a group of intrepid skiers negotiat-

ing harrowing precipices above Chamonix; down a steep country road at the head of a pack of bicycle racers; up to the highest gargoyle standing guard over majestic Mont-Saint-Michel; below the earth in a cool wine cellar; back to sea level on a bikini-bedecked dock at Cannes; into a cathedral; out of a walled fishing village; and finally up the Eiffel Tower from the unique viewpoint of a camera making the dizzy ascent on the *roof* of one of the elevators!

And now, back to the streets of the city/village, perhaps for a last sip of wine at the sidewalk café or a final stroll along the Seine. If it's nighttime, there quite possibly will be a fireworks display over the lagoon, reminiscent of a Bastille Day celebration (the French equivalent of America's Independence Day, held on July 14). Sequenced lighting of all the buildings and streets will re-create the twinkling brilliance of the singular "City of Lights."

Germany

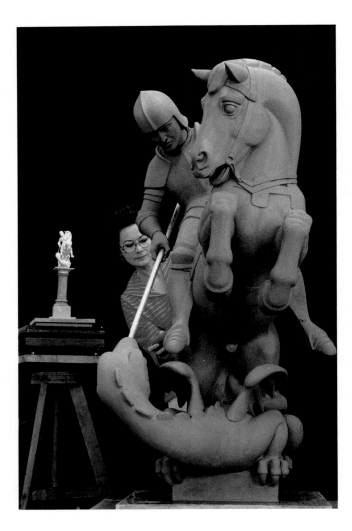

Yes, we think of fairy tales when we daydream about Germany, and of craftsmanship, of the romance of the river castles, of oompah bands, and of sauerkraut and beer. And they're all here in the Germany pavilion of Epcot Center's World Showcase.

We stroll over cobblestones to the center of the town *platz* with its statue of St. George slaying the dragon, a favorite German theme. This one was modeled after the one in Rothenburg.

In the studio at WED, left, a sculptor puts the finishing touches on St. George and the Dragon for Germany's platz. Note that the small model in the background and the completed statue differ in pose from the version in the artist's earlier painting, above, which is pictured in front of the clock tower.

A number of craft shops, quaint in concept, appealing in content, front the *platz*. One shop displays and sells clocks and other mechanical crafts, including handmade music boxes. Another offers a variety of German wines that visitors may taste before making a selection.

In Glaz und Porzellan, the Goebel-Hummel ceramic shop, a demonstration area has been set apart where visitors can see artists painting the exquisite figurines, and, of course, there will be a selection of Hummels for sale.

In Porzellanhaus, a store with octagonal vaulted ceilings, there are displays of porcelain wares, including place settings and other utilitarian merchandise as well as fantastic figures of birds and animals.

But the family favorite is sure to be the toyshop, Der Teddybär. Its carved wood interior sets off displays of train models, dolls, miniature castles, and a menagerie of the world-renowned stuffed animals by Steiff.

The tourism area, when it is completed, will convey the feeling of a medieval town hall with suits of armor, coats of arms of Germany's states and cities, and other appropriate and well-researched appointments.

The future River Ride promises to be as enjoyable as it is informative. An early concept has visitors boarding a "cruise boat" for a simulated ride down the Rhine and other rivers, the trip affording a visual impression in miniature of the cultural heritage of Germany's past and the highlights of its present.

What is in place, though, and larger than life, is the Biergarten, to most tourists an essential part of their visit to Germany. And what a beer garden!

Three stories high, with tables placed around a

The picturesque architecture of an old German city surrounds the cobbled Platz *of the Germany pavilion.*

The Oktoberfest is in full swing, with the oompah band playing, while happy visitors quaff the best German lager and beat time on the tables—wishing they never had to leave.

tiered semicircle, the indoor garden miraculously conveys the feeling of an outdoor courtyard. In one corner is a tree, in another a full-sized, functioning waterwheel.

On the opposite side of the garden is a meticulous re-creation of the best of sixteenth-century Rothenburg, complete with its residences. In the center of the town square is a stage where live entertainers, including that inevitable and beloved oompah band, dance and sing and make German music.

Served with the best German beers are such traditional tidbits as bratwurst, sauerkraut, potato dumplings, hot pretzels, sauerbraten, smoked pork in aspic, sausage . . . everything that is Teutonic and tasty.

The setting is simply splendid, the sort of place we would all love to visit, and many will be loath to leave the jollity of the Biergarten. But leave we must, back to the *platz* for a last look around, while the glockenspielers halfway up the clock tower chime the hour and the band thumps out a final chorus of a rollicking polka.

Perhaps the lights are coming on now, illuminating the windows and louvers, the edge of a chimney, the rustic wooden balconies and beams of this charming town, and making it such a place of enchantment that it is even harder to depart. Maybe we can leave a little trail of breadcrumbs— or pretzel crumbs—as Hansel and Gretel did, to ensure our return.

At dusk, the torii, Japan's ceremonial gate of honor, is silhouetted against the Florida sky.

Among design details specially executed for the pavilion are hangings with stylized chrysanthemum motifs, above right.

Japan

Underlying modern Japan's high-tech hustle and bustle are its enduring traditions, characterized by grace, refinement, serenity, formality, taste, proportion, decorum, delicacy. And to a remarkable degree, these, too, are the qualities reflected in Epcot Center's Japan. It would be wise, then, to bow to another honored Japanese custom: bring a camera and plenty of film.

The approach to Japan is dramatic. In the lagoon is a replica of the ancient Itsukushima Shrine on an island in the Inland Sea, and in the water beyond the shore stands a vermilion *torii*, a gate of honor resembling a Japanese calligraphic character.

Facing the pavilion grounds, one sees a sight to stir the imagination. Flanking the entrance to the left is the graceful *goju-no-to*, or five-story pagoda,

whose stages, in ascending order, represent the elements from which Buddhists believe all things in the universe are created: earth, water, fire, wind, and sky. Inspired by the exquisite eighth-century pagoda of Horyuji temple in Nara, it stands eighty-three feet high. The roof is surmounted by a *sorin*, a spire composed of nine rings, each with its own wind chimes, and topped by a water flame, and, since this is Florida and not Japan, a lightning rod.

Walking clockwise around the square, we enter a formal garden conceived as an oasis of serenity. A meandering stream tumbles over a waterfall and flows under several rustic footbridges to end in a *koi*-fish pond. Along the way it rambles past formal arrangements of flowers, rocks, lanterns, paths, and pebbles that appeal not only to the eyes but to all the senses—save, perhaps, that of taste.

The Japan pavilion's skeleton, above, while taking shape at Epcot Center, had a remarkable elegance foretelling the beauty of the finished buildings. Now the goju-no-to, *or five-story pagoda at right, is illuminated at night like some gorgeous Japanese lantern.*

This last has not been overlooked by a country whose cuisine has attracted more and more chopstick gourmets. At the top of the gently sloping garden, not far from the waterfall, stands a teahouse, a small version of part of the Katsura imperial villa in the Kyoto gardens, which serves here as a restaurant offering Japanese snacks.

Japan pavilion's show, when it is ready, will afford an unparalleled overview of Japanese history. Entitled "Meet the World," it will also be the feature attraction of Tokyo Disneyland.

The first chapter traces the volcanic origin of the islands. Then, in the company of two Japanese children and an animated magical crane (symbol of good health and long life), we explore the history of the inhabitants of the islands.

The show ends with the children and the crane waving farewell from the gondola of a balloon. But we can return to Japan, at least for a moment, after we leave the theater: it is there all around us, and our appreciation will be heightened after what we have just seen.

"Meet the World," the Japan pavilion's show, will include the Great Buddha at Nara, above left, and a scene from the twelfth-century Tale of Genji, below left. The torii, below, welcomes visitors from across the water.

Italy

The heart of every Italian village, and of many big-city neighborhoods as well, is the piazza. It is like an outdoor room, with space for strolling, for people-watching, and for sitting at sidewalk tables over an espresso or an aperitif. Not surprisingly, the designers of Italy decided that the centerpiece of this pavilion would be the quintessential Italian piazza.

The first thing you notice is the color. This pavilion is the color of Italy—unduplicated anywhere in the world, not even in Mediterranean Spain or Greece—a warm umber with tones of yellow and red. Add to this the good Italian smells coming from the kitchen of Alfredo's restaurant on the piazza, and the essence of Italy instantly surrounds you.

From the vantage point of a little island, surrounded by a canal cut from the lagoon to give the feel of Venice (and outfitted with several gondolas moored to those familiar "barber poles"), you get an excellent view of the entire pavilion. Dominating the scene to the left are replicas of Venice's fourteenth-century Doge's Palace and, next to it, the thousand-year-old campanile, or bell tower, scaled down but still one hundred feet high. And what attention to detail has been lavished on the palace, for many centuries one of the architectural gems of the Queen of the Adriatic!

There is a wealth of detail in all the buildings that perhaps only a doge or a Venetian angel could fully appreciate. Taken as a whole, it contributes immensely to the pavilion's air of authenticity—even if there are no pigeons in Epcot's version of St. Mark's Square. But the products sold on the ground floor of the palace are completely authentic Venetian imports—Venetian glass, crystal, and jewelry.

From the palace you might go next door to sip an espresso or a Campari on the open terrace of Alfredo's. This version of the renowned *ristorante* in Rome is designed in the Florentine style, both outside and inside. Truly an elegant place, it has borrowed the rich colors of Renaissance fabrics and carpeting. The only reminders of the restaurant's prototype are the lobby, its walls covered with photographs of the famous, and the kitchen, its chefs faithfully reproducing the cuisine that originally drew celebrities to Alfredo's, where their pasta was served with golden forks.

But here the restaurant walls vie with the pasta for the attention of the guests. No ordinary walls, these are based on Veronese's remarkable perspective paintings. The trick is called *trompe l'oeil,* and it fools the eye indeed. One wall features court musicians who look so real that you'll strain to hear their music. The east wall depicts a view from a terrace overlooking a Florentine landscape, while at the south end, the wall is punctuated by three doors through which restaurant staff comes and goes. It is only when you become aware that Alfredo's waiters pass through just the center door that you realize the rest of the crew are painted figures.

The Italy pavilion's waterfront is a replica of Venice, startlingly like the actual city, with the Doge's Palace and campanile waiting to be photographed by Epcot Center's tourists.

The great Neptune, right, will undoubtedly cut an impressive figure as the centerpiece of Italy's magnificent fountain.

Leaving Alfredo's, well satisfied but a little perplexed by the painted tricks, you stroll around the far end of the piazza, past garden walls behind which a stand of stone Roman pines seems to whisper ancient tales of Romulus and Remus.

Next, you come to the fountain, without which a piazza simply isn't a piazza. And this one isn't just a small model. Watching over your three coins and his own retinue of water-spouting dolphins is the heroic figure of the sea god, sculpted in the style of Bernini, and surely modeled after the great Neptune himself.

On the colorful raised platform in the center of the piazza, meanwhile, there's probably some form of entertainment going on. You might stop and take a seat to watch folk dancing, or a performance of *commedia dell'arte*, the improvisatory theater born in the Middle Ages, or a puppet show. *Commedia dell'arte* was the ancestor of the Renaissance Punch and Judy show, which also originated in Italy.

Then, completing the circuit, you might pause for a little impulse shopping, choosing among the leather goods, basketry, and ceramics at the pavilion's Northern Italy building. This structure, reminiscent of a typical market-square city hall of the fifteenth or sixteenth century (and modeled perhaps most closely on a similar building in Bergamo), is, in some ways, the most engaging in the Italy pavilion. Its designers have included the small incongruities and oddities that give an old building a history, adding to its charm. Few buildings remain perfectly preserved as they were when new. Over the centuries, landlords change; one year they are prosperous, and they build on additions. The next year they're a little short of funds, so they tear down part of the structure and sell the stones.

In a sense, the Italy pavilion itself is a victim of this cycle of fortune; the area which was to represent Southern Italy—not to mention a splendid replica of Roman ruins—may not be completed until 1983.

Meanwhile, the pavilion as it now stands will amply reward you with its colors, its gaiety, its genuine flavor of Italy.

China

These graceful stylized dragons—unmistakably Chinese—are part of the decorative scheme designed for the pagoda's exterior beams.

As you pass through the ceremonial gate of China, you will see ahead of you an exquisite structure styled after the Temple of Heaven in Peking, the focal point of the pavilion grounds.

As a first step, contemplate the three imposing rocks by the entrance to China, each about fifteen feet high. Centuries ago, the Chinese learned that contemplation of the shape and texture of particularly lovely rock forms contributes to the serenity of one's nature.

The lotus pool is another inducement to serenity. After gazing at the floating waterlilies and tiny waterfall, cross the graceful bridge over the pool and enter the three-tiered round temple.

Your next stop is a pre-show area where a display of photographs is planned. Through the windows, you also will get a tantalizing invitation to visit an adjacent art gallery. But now you are ushered into the theater to view a remarkable film on China.

The film will show all the classic sights long hidden from Western eyes: the Great Wall, the

Republic of China

y Concept Design

1 13, 1981

This early rendering gives an idea of what China will look like to visitors arriving by boat.

Forbidden City, the Summer Palace, the Yangtze River, the Leshan Buddha near Chengdu in Sichuan Province, and the excavation of the Qin Shi Huang Tomb, where row upon row of life-size clay warriors and horses have stood guard for centuries.

From here, you might seek out the art gallery glimpsed from the pre-show area, or take a picture in front of the tall, thin pagoda near a reflecting pool, or meander through a garden and contemplate a good Chinese dinner.

The Disney filmmakers were the first foreigners permitted to photograph Tibet's capital, Lhasa. The magnificent Potala Palace, left, once the seat of the Dalai Lamas, occupies an entire hill overlooking the city.

The essence of old China has been captured in its pavilion, above. The three-story Temple of Heaven, the lotus pool in the foreground, the distinctive landscaping and spacious courtyard all give the visitor a real sense of the country.

United Kingdom

It begins and ends with a pub, the United Kingdom pavilion, a happy reaffirmation of the wit and wisdom of Sydney Smith, who wrote over a century ago, "What two ideas are more inseparable than beer and Britannia?" Let's drink to that with a pint of bitter before venturing out in the midday sun for a leisurely amble through the United Kingdom of World Showcase.

It is possible to tour the United Kingdom by walking through the shops up one side of High Street and down Tudor Lane without once stepping outside, savoring the flavor of Britain just from the interiors, so painstaking has been the designers' work. High Street, Tudor Lane, and Upper and Lower Regency streets are lined with stores and more stores. It is not without justification that the United Kingdom has been called a nation of shopkeepers.

The Rose and Crown, left, is one jolly little corner that will forever England be. Visitors discover here why pubs are a favorite British institution. In the rendering at right, the United Kingdom's cheery lights are reflected in the lagoon.

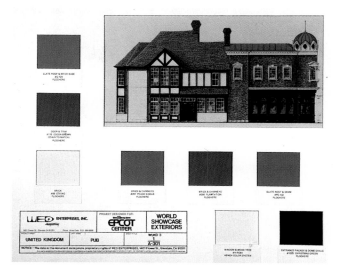

The colorboard, above, for one of the facades of the Rose and Crown illustrates the careful attention to detail that resulted in the faithful recreation of this bit of England.

High Street, left, offers a colorful mix of English architectural styles—Elizabethan, Tudor, and Victorian. But it is the Cockney "Pearlies" whose music and dancing enliven the street scene.

And what a collection of shops to browse through! On the left corner of High Street as you leave the pub is a Cotswold cottage, resembling Anne Hathaway's in Stratford-upon-Avon.

Continuing along High Street to Tudor Lane, your way takes you, from building to building, through a broad sampling of British merchandise —from simple biscuits to luxurious Royal Doulton china. The wares become increasingly sophisticated (and expensive) as you advance. At the same time, as you go from one shop to the next, you are moving through a range of English architectural styles.

Ending at the pub where you began your tour, you might stop there again, this time for a stirrup cup.

Africa

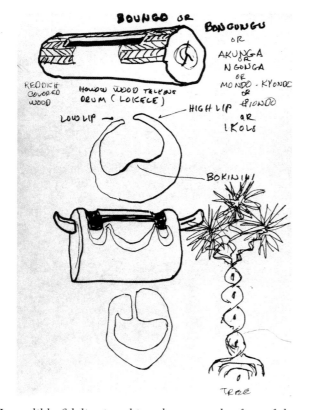

Incredible fidelity is achieved as a result of careful homework done on every detail of a presentation. These rough sketches for a display on the history of the drum, the pre-show to "The Heartbeat of Africa," document several instruments.

There is an ever-expanding number of pavilions to be incorporated into the World Showcase complex, some already in the planning stages.

Farthest along in concept is the African Nations pavilion, unique among World Showcase projects in that it is not devoted to any single country but to all of those in Africa that lie, roughly, across the equatorial belt.

The pavilion will offer a comprehensive view of the "dark continent." Its architectural motif is a tree house, in which visitors will overlook a jungle water hole in a simulated nighttime environment. The illusion of the jungle will be heightened by a remarkably authentic diorama of trees, vines, boulders, and rushing water; even the scents of the forest will be re-created. These actual objects, sounds, and smells are blended skillfully with a rear-projected film of animals visiting the water hole to convince visitors that they are actually in the heart of Africa.

One of the pavilion's shows is called "The Heartbeat of Africa." In the pre-show area, dedicated to the history of the drum, an African narrator and actual instruments vividly demonstrate its significance to the African culture.

The show itself will trace the history of Equatorial Africa—its past, its present, and a glimpse of its future—through the eyes of a traditional griot, or storyteller. The filmed presentation will be not only an engaging entertainment but also a learning experience. The show will culminate with an outdoor jazz concert filmed in a modern African city, the excitement building up as superimposed laser images begin to emanate from the instruments themselves.

In the Heritage area, an African village that is an amalgam of the styles of various countries and

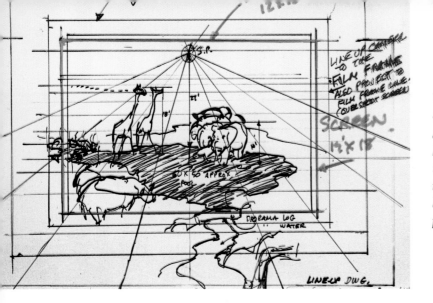

When the Africa pavilion opens, visitors will be enthralled by the film sequence of animals coming to drink at a jungle water hole. Its effectiveness is due in large part to the painstaking thoroughness that went into the planning of the shot. At left is the layout, and below the rendering; in the pavilion the experience itself awaits you.

In the Heritage area, authentic traditional performers vividly enact village life in Equatorial Africa.

regions will give the visitor a broad general experience of the daily life of the African. Authentically traditional performers, in a live demonstration, will present their cultural heritage as the area's entertainment. A museum is planned to house a permanent exhibit of fine African art, with additional sculptures and paintings occasionally loaned by various African countries.

A second show, "Africa Rediscovered," will be a key attraction of the pavilion. A pre-show area, dominated by a large relief map of the continent, will graphically and entertainingly limn the geography of Africa, its flora and fauna, climate, and other information of interest.

The show, on film, will be hosted by Alex Haley, author of *Roots*, who has acted as adviser to the pavilion.

Mexico

Can any country under the sun be as rich in lore as Mexico? Was there ever a past as tumultuous, a present as colorful, a future as promising? The possibility will seem remote after a tour through the Mexico pavilion.

Epcot's Mexico, quite literally a labor of love, is unique among World Showcase pavilions in several respects:

- Except for an informal café on the lagoon and the towering pyramid that is the pavilion's architectural theme, the entire area is enclosed.

- A major part of the story of Mexico is told through the medium of the dance, a device as engaging as it is unusual.

- Most of the pavilion's design and staging crew are Mexican-Americans, whose pride in their heritage is mirrored in their presentation.

Although the excursion through "Las Tres Culturas de México" inside the pavilion is the highlight of the presentation, the signature and symbol of Mexico is the imposing pyramid temple at the entrance. Rising thirty-six feet above the lagoon in a series of steps, the structure combines elements of ancient Mesoamerican civilizations that go back to the third century A.D.

Inside the pavilion, we enjoy the vista over a slope, across a bustling plaza, past an "outdoor" restaurant to a small lagoon that is both entrance

The entrance to Mexico's pavilion is through this towering Mayan pyramid that seems to have stood here for centuries.

A dancer costumed as the Spirit of Water in the dance of "The Four Elements" has her makeup put on. The costume sketch for the Spirit of Water, right, details the goddess's elaborate headdress.

As visitors approach the entrance to the ride-through attraction, they will pass this large Olmec head, left. The Olmec culture is considered the "mother culture" of ancient Mexico.

to the ride and focal point of the panoramic view—all of this, incredibly, is indoors!

The plaza is lined on two sides with shops like those found in almost any Mexican village or town, although the designers took their example from Taxco, one of Mexico's most beautiful old settlements. In Colonial buildings with flower-decked wrought-iron balconies, tile roofs, hand-painted signs, and outdoor staircases, visitors may browse or buy jewelry, sombreros, dresses, serapes, silver goods, and other souvenirs.

From the dining terrace or from the plaza,

The sketches opposite and below are for the dance that shows the struggle between Quetzalcóatl, who represents good, and Tezcatlipoca, the god of evil. The Aztec warriors at right—Eagle, Bear, and Jaguar—dance out a story.

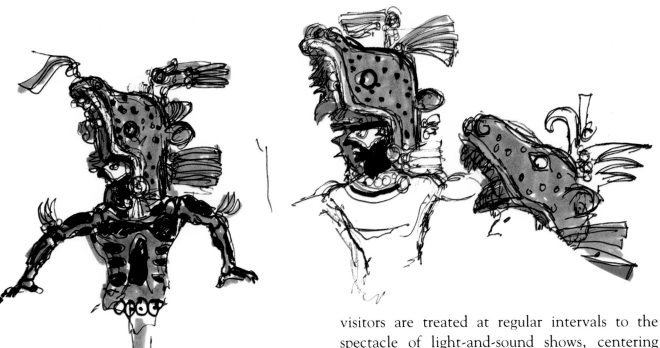

visitors are treated at regular intervals to the spectacle of light-and-sound shows, centering on the small lagoon. Across the water is another pyramid, ancient and crumbling, and a large stone Olmec head. This is the entrance to "The Three Cultures of Mexico." Pre-Columbian Mexico comes to life in a series of ancient dances.

The Quetzalcóatl and Tezcatlipoca sequence

Colorful lighting dramatizes the small model of a Mayan pyramid at WED. In the pavilion this is where visitors board boats for a spectacular excursion through "The Three Cultures of Mexico."

symbolizes the eternal struggle between good and evil. Quetzalcóatl, the feathered serpent, is the god of light, wisdom, and virtue, while his opponent is the tiger god of evil, ignorance, and darkness, a duality that fascinated the pre-Columbian peoples.

The Spanish Colonial period is presented as a kaleidoscope of doll-sized Audio-Animatronics figures in regional folk costumes, dancing, singing, and playing music. The fiestas of Mexico are celebrated in a glorious gambol that seems to embrace us all in its exuberance.

It is the nation's rich past that has most captivated the Mexican-Americans who contributed to the show so unsparingly, and who summed it up so well. "We found out much about the history, the people: the mother culture of the Olmecs; then the Mayas, who were our equivalent of the Greeks; the Toltecs, our Etruscans; the Aztecs, our Romans. And then, to be able to communicate the whole story through music, dancing, color, and texture—a universal language . . . We hated to see it end."

"We hated to see it end." Visitors to Epcot, after touring Future World and World Showcase, are likely to echo those words. They will also come away with something of the feeling so aptly expressed by Walter Cronkite:

This universality of Disney carries on after his death, and continues in projects that he had put on the drawing board before he died. Epcot Center in Florida is a case in point—bringing together representatives of international industry, international commerce, and the governments of other countries in a permanent world's fair. It perpetuates that theme of his that we are indeed one people.

At night the plaza takes on the atmosphere of a typical Mexican village with outdoor vendors and strolling mariachis adding to the gaiety.

This book is dedicated to, and inspired by, Walt Disney's vision of a world where human freedom, enterprise, and imagination combine to create an international community of people and ideas, fact and future, probable and possible, challenge and choice.

Walt Disney's Epcot chronicles a twenty-year dream, now come true through the unique blending of Disney talents—artist and designer, engineer and technician—with hundreds of advisors and consultants and thousands of construction workers. All have invested their abilities—and more than 25 million hours from dream to reality—in Walt Disney's concept. May Epcot forever be a source of joy, inspiration, hope and new knowledge to those who come here from across America and around the world.